I0426034

Shoreline Change Monitoring at Fire Island National Seashore

2008-2009 Annual Report

Natural Resource Technical Report NPS/NCBN/NRTR—2011/515

Norbert P. Psuty
William Hudacek
Aaron Love
Tanya M. Silveira

Institute of Marine and Coastal Sciences
Rutgers - The State University of New Jersey
74 Magruder Road
Highlands, New Jersey 07732

December 2011

U.S. Department of the Interior
National Park Service
Natural Resource Stewardship and Science
Fort Collins, Colorado

The National Park Service, Natural Resource Stewardship and Science office in Fort Collins, Colorado publishes a range of reports that address natural resource topics of interest and applicability to a broad audience in the National Park Service and others in natural resource management, including scientists, conservation and environmental constituencies, and the public.

The Natural Resource Technical Report Series is used to disseminate results of scientific studies in the physical, biological, and social sciences for both the advancement of science and the achievement of the National Park Service mission. The series provides contributors with a forum for displaying comprehensive data that are often deleted from journals because of page limitations.

All manuscripts in the series receive the appropriate level of peer review to ensure that the information is scientifically credible, technically accurate, appropriately written for the intended audience, and designed and published in a professional manner.

Data in this report were collected and analyzed using methods based on established, peer-reviewed protocols and were analyzed and interpreted within the guidelines of the protocols.

Views, statements, findings, conclusions, recommendations, and data in this report do not necessarily reflect views and policies of the National Park Service, U.S. Department of the Interior. Mention of trade names or commercial products does not constitute endorsement or recommendation for use by the U.S. Government.

This report is available from the Northeast Coastal and Barrier Network website (http://science.nature.nps.gov/im/units/ncbn/) and the Natural Resource Publications Management website (http://www.nature.nps.gov/publications/nrpm/).

Please cite this publication as:

Psuty, N. P., W. Hudacek, A. Love, T. M. Silveira. 2011. Shoreline change monitoring at Fire Island National Seashore: 2008-2009 annual report. Natural Resource Technical Report NPS/NCBN/NRTR—2011/515. National Park Service, Fort Collins, Colorado.

NPS 615/111995, December 2011

Contents

Figures

Figures (continued)

Tables

Executive Summary

This annual report documents the collection of shoreline position data and describes the short-term variation that has occurred during the period from Spring 2008 to Spring 2009 in the Fire Island barrier island, including elements of the Fire Island National Seashore, as called for in the Northeast Coastal and Barrier Network's protocol on shoreline monitoring (Psuty, et al., 2010). The changes in shoreline position are generally descriptive of the seasonal contrasts (lower energetics in the summer period versus higher energetics in the winter period) that support sediment accumulation during summer and erosion during the winter. However, there are many natural variables and cultural events that affect the gains and losses of sediment and the displacements of the beach. The 1D shoreline surveys were conducted in March 2008, October 2008, and March 2009. They incorporate changes caused by a major beach nourishment project in many of the communities and a county project to place sediment dredged from Moriches Inlet along a portion of Smith Point County Park. As a result, most of the communities had a net positive shoreline displacement (mean of 3.2 m) and some of the County Park had a net positive shoreline displacement for the year. However, most of the NPS land and the State Park had a net inland displacement, -3.61 m and -14.87 m, respectively. The mean shoreline position change for the annual period, Spring 2008 to Spring 2009, for the entire island was an inland displacement, -3.66 m.

This annual report on shoreline position change of the Fire Island ocean shoreline does offer some insight into the areas of coastal dynamics and sediment budget. However, it is report on only one year of observations and does not establish a trend. The protocols for shoreline monitoring created a comparable geodatabase that will lead to efficiencies in data assembly and analysis.

Acknowledgments

The field survey team is a critical component in the gathering of the field data and the subsequent processing of the data sets. Particular recognition is given to Dennis Skidds (Data Manager, Northeast Coastal & Barrier Network), Jordan Raphael (Park Biologist, Fire Island National Seashore), and Jason Flynn (Park Ranger, Fire Island National Seashore) for conducting shoreline position surveys and in cleaning up the collected data files. The shoreline monitoring could not have occurred without the able logistical assistance of Park personnel, Jordan Raphael and Michael Bilecki (Chief of Resources Management, Fire Island National Seashore), in the provision of onsite assistance and encouragement. Robin Baranowski, Northeast Coastal and Barrier Network, provided constructive and valuable assistance in the final production of this report.

This project is supported by the Northeast Coastal and Barrier Network of the National Park Service Inventory and Monitoring Program (Sara Stevens, NCBN Program Manager). It is carried out under Cooperative Agreement CA4520-99-007, Task Order J4506040626/0005.

Introduction

This is one of a series of Annual Reports of the change in shoreline position along the ocean side of Fire Island from inlet to inlet. This report follows the protocols on monitoring described in Psuty, et al. (2009) that were applied for the first time on Fire Island in the Fall of 2005. Subsequent surveys conducted in the spring of 2008, the fall of 2008, and the spring of 2009 provide the temporal span for this annual report.

The goal of the annual report is to document the collection of the shoreline position data and to describe the short-term variation that has occurred. The changes in position are generally descriptive of the seasonal contrasts (lower energetics in the summer period versus higher energetics in the winter period) that support accumulation during summer and erosion during the winter. However, there are many other variables that affect the gains and losses of sediment and the displacements of the beach, especially along a barrier island, such as Fire Island. Therefore, the short-term annual report is but the first step in the understanding of the conditions that characterize the island and is meant to establish a baseline of information for subsequent characterization and analyses. Discussions and analyses of vectors of shoreline change and likely associations will be the theme of the longer-term (5 years) Trend Reports.

Site and Situation

Fire Island is a barrier island along the southern coast of Long Island, New York (Fig. 1). The barrier is approximately 50 km alongshore from Moriches Inlet to Fire Island Inlet. Each of the inlets is controlled by the presence of jetties bordering federally-maintained navigation channels. Whereas the Moriches Inlet terminus of Fire Island is relatively stable in position because of the pair of jetties defining the channel position, the Fire Island Inlet terminus of Fire Island (Democrat Point) extends considerably beyond the single western jetty and is quite mobile.

Each of the seasonal surveys records the position of the shoreline at that time and subsequent surveys compare the changing position through time and space. The resulting data set is a measure of change for specific portions of developed and undeveloped portions of the island as well as larger groupings of administrative units of the barrier island.

For Fire Island, the area of special interest consists of the holdings of the 17 communities that share presence on the island, as well as the other park jurisdictions (Robert Moses State Park and Smith Point County Park) (Fig. 1). Particular portions of these areas may be designated for special attention at a later time.

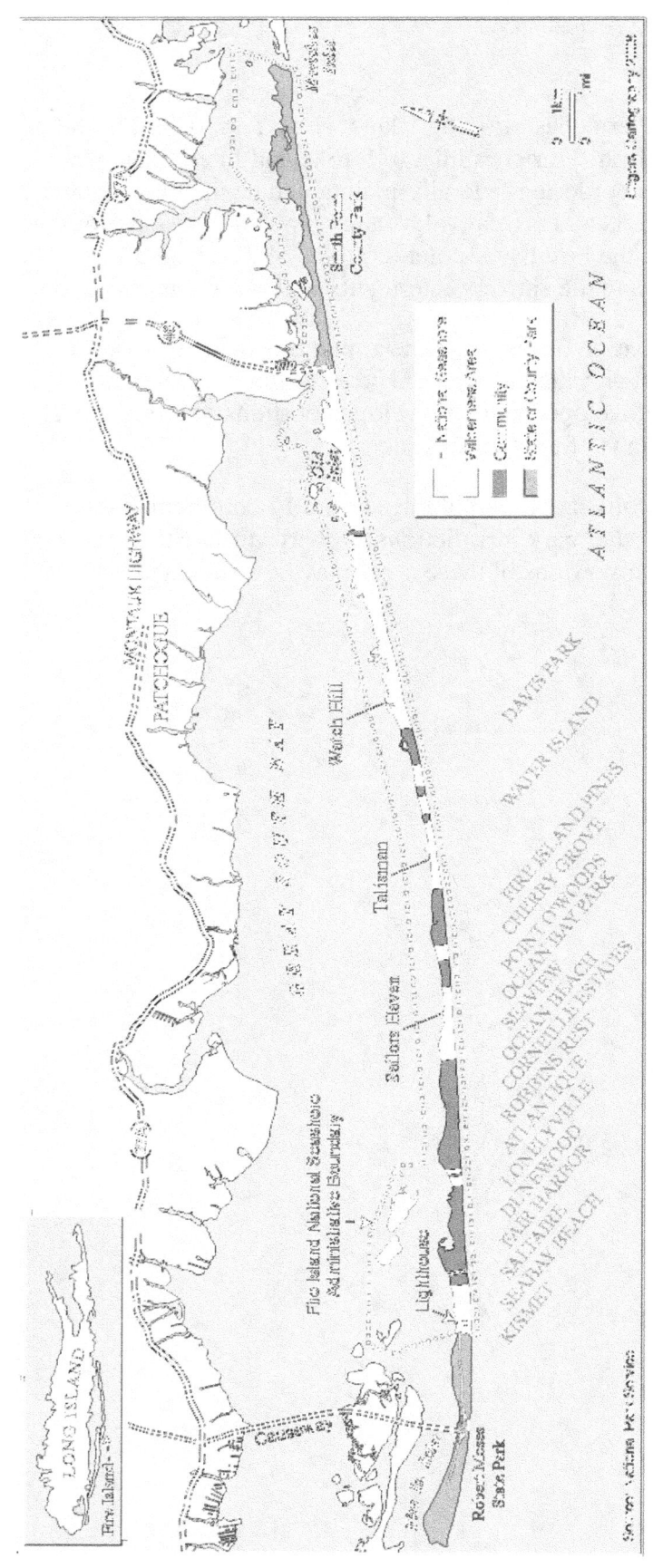

Figure 1. Fire Island, the communities, and the administrative units present on the barrier island.

4

Timing of Shoreline Position Surveys

Three surveys of the neap-tide, high-tide swash-line are included in this annual report (Table 1). They represent the positions monitored from the Spring of 2008 to the Spring of 2009. The three surveys were run during the predicted neap-tide period and had similar water level elevations.

There is no ocean tide gauge located on Fire Island. There are secondary gauges in Great South Bay and at the inland margins of the two inlets. However, they are in locations of restricted tidal amplitude compared to the ocean tidal range and thus are not good indicators of the water position on the ocean beach, nor the timing of high water at the beach. The nearest gauge that portrays the ocean condition is at the northern end of Sandy Hook, NOAA National Ocean Data Center, Station 8531680 (NOAA, 2009). This gauge is used to reference water level positions and the timing of the water levels in this report. Sandy Hook is also the gauge used to predict water level variation for the general Fire Island area by the NOAA National Ocean Data Center.

Table 1. Date of shoreline survey and elevation of previous high tide.

Season	Date	Previous High Tide	
		Height* (m)	Time
Spring 2008	17 March 2008	1.527	04:06am
Fall 2008	9 October 2008	1.191	02:30am
Spring 2009	23 March 2009	1.428	05:18am

*Tide heights relative to Mean Lower Low Water, Sandy Hook

Natural and Cultural Events Affecting Shoreline Position

Natural Events

Storms are important elements of the environment that affect shoreline position by mobilizing and transporting beach and dune sediment. The existing protocol for shoreline monitoring is directed at identifying the seasonal, annual, and longer sediment balances at the ocean shoreline by recording changing positions of the water-land contact. Individual storms create short-term variations in the beach position and can be accommodated by judicious planning of survey dates to avoid periods of short-term storm erosion and recovery, and to emphasize neap-tide swash positions independent of specific storms.

Storms are a condition at the ocean beach. They are important drivers of coastal change. However, the absence of an ocean tide gauge at or near Fire Island causes this report to consider other means to identify the temporal distribution and the magnitude of storm events shaping beach position. Whereas the Sandy Hook tide gauge was a good resource for the determination of neap tide occurrence and elevation, it lacked the exposure to respond to the full range of ambient wave directions and storm surges that approach and affect Fire Island. The Sandy Hook tide gauge does provide some insight into storm events from the eastern and southern sectors. However, it does not do justice to waves and surge from the southwest and west. In an effort to identify the range of coastal storms that affect the Fire Island area, wave data from an offshore buoy have been reviewed to describe conditions of storminess and relative intensity and duration. These wave data are derived from the NOAA National Data Buoy Center and apply to Station 44025 (located about 45 km southeast of Moriches Inlet, NY (NOAA, 2009), supplemented by data from Station 44017 because of gaps in the Station 44025 record.

Wave data are often described by statistical values such as wave height, wave length, wave period, etc. A common wave descriptor is "significant wave height", which is the mean of the highest one-third of the waves measured during some time interval. In the case of NOAA Station 44025, significant wave heights were determined for successive 20 minute intervals and plotted to describe the sequence of wave conditions during January 2008 through April 2009 (Fig. 2). Periods of large significant wave heights were associated with storm events and the wave data were screened to establish threshold conditions. It was determined that a minimum significant wave height of 3 m would be used to identify the number and the duration of the storm events.

Using this method, 39 storms have been identified as occurring between the beginning of January 2008 and the end of April 2009 (Table 2). Further, durations of the storm events were established by noting consecutive dates with greater than 3 m significant wave height for the 20 minute periods, describing storms of 1-4 days in duration (Table 2). In addition to wave height, the NOAA offshore buoy also records wave direction, in azimuth degrees, from which the waves are arriving (Table 2) (Station 44017 does not record wave direction and thus that variable is absent from Table 2 if a storm occurred during one of the data gaps).

The combination of data in Figure 2 and Table 2 portrays the winter, spring, and fall seasons as the times of most numerous and most severe storm events, with the May 12-13 storm having a significant wave height of 5.27 m (only slightly greater that the September 6-7 storm significant wave height of 5.24 m. The December 19-22 storm was a severe event with a maximum significant wave height of 4.2 m, with a duration of 38 hours, and lasting through two high tides.

The late spring and summer period are times of lower waves, storm threshold was not exceeded, and presumably lower rates of sediment transport and loss.

Because the shoreline position surveys are scheduled at six-month intervals, they are not meant to represent the outcomes of specific storms, but instead they should provide insight into the comparison of times of high energy levels and considerable sediment transport relative to those times of lower energy levels and more opportunity for sediment retention. Yet, the results may not be so simple. There are other variables at work that affect the outcomes, such as the local sites of sediment accumulation and loss associated with the structures at the inlets and along the shoreline; human manipulation of sediment; inshore circulation cells that add the dimensions of current patterns to the sediment mobility equation, alongshore transfers of pulses of sediment, etc.

Cultural Events/Emplacement of Sediment

The period in this report included the emplacement of 21,000 m^3 of sediment to the foredune area amongst the houses in Davis Park (during March and April, 2008). The sediment was quarried from outside of the barrier island and thus introduced new sediment to the general sediment supply. However, the sand was placed high on the profile, early in the survey period. It is unlikely to have caused shoreline displacement.

A major beach nourishment project was conducted from January 2009 through April 2009 and it directly displaced the shoreline in the communities from Davis Park to Saltaire. Approximately 1.39 million m^3 of sediment was dredged from offshore sources and pumped to the beaches in the communities. Although the sediment was not placed directly on the NPS lands, the alongshore transport effectively contributed to shoreline accumulation in areas between the nourished community beaches, and downdrift beyond Saltaire. Additionally, in late 2008 and early 2009, 238,000 m^3 of sediment was dredged from the navigation channel at Moriches Inlet and placed along two beach units at Smith Point County Park, approximately 58,000 m^3 at the Pavilion and 180,000 m^3 in an area between the Pavilion and Moriches Inlet. This sediment displaced the shoreline in the County Park and contributed sediment downdrift to the National Seashore.

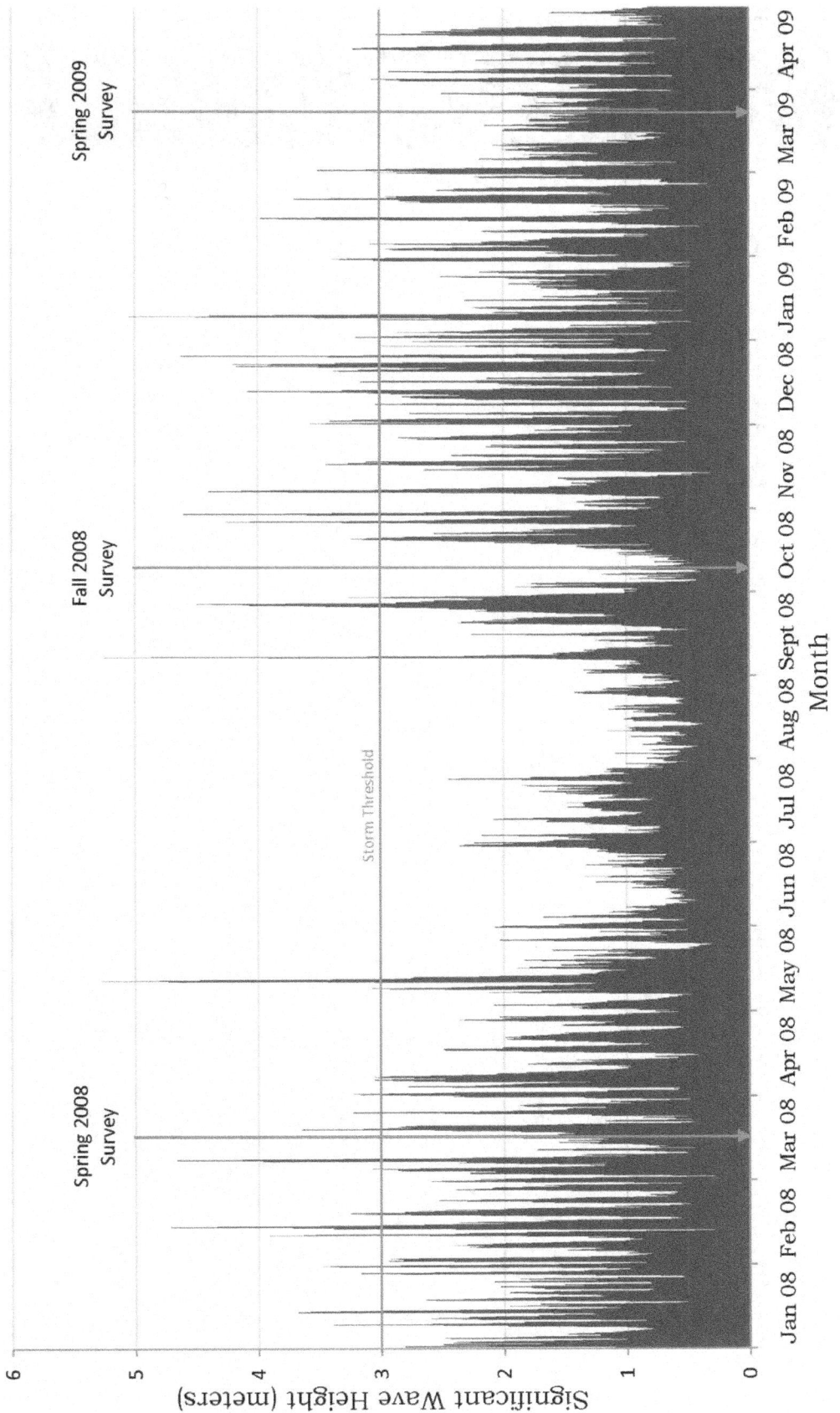

Figure 2. Distribution of significant wave heights from January 2008 through April 2009; establishment of storm threshold and storm events; and timing of shoreline surveys (source: NOAA Ocean Data Center, Buoys 44025 and 44017).

Table 2. Storm events - January 2008 through April 2009 (NOAA, 2011).

Period	Maximum Significant Wave Height (m)	Average Wave Direction (Quadrant)	Duration (Hours)	Number of High Tides
9 Jan 2008	3.39	unreported	4	1
14 Jan 2008	3.68	unreported	14	1
28 Jan 2008	3.17	E	2	0
30 Jan 2008	3.48	S	9	0
10-11 Feb 2008	3.91	W	8	1
13-14 Feb 2008	4.71	S	23	2
18 Feb 2008	3.25	SE	5	0
5-6 Mar 2008	3.07	S	2	0
8-9 Mar 2008	4.66	S	21	1
20 Mar 2008	3.65	S	7	1
26 Mar 2008	3.23	S	4	1
1-2 Apr 2008	3.23	S	5	0
7-8 Apr 2008	3.05	E	6	0
9 May 2008	3.07	E	1	0
12-13 May 2008	5.27	E	25	2
6-7 Sep 2008	5.24	S	9	1
25-26 Sep 2008	4.49	SE	31	2
28 Sep 2008	3.26	SE	2	0
19-20 Oct 2008	3.24	E	8	0
25-26 Oct 2008	4.26	SE	11	1
28-29 Oct 2008	4.6	W	13	2
5-6 Nov 2008	4.4	SE	22	2
16-17 Nov 2008	3.44	SW	7	0
30 Nov - 2 Dec 2008	3.57	SE	12	2
7 Dec 2008	3.04	W	1	0
11-12 Dec 2008	4.08	SE	21	2
16 Dec 2008	3.16	unreported	2	0
19-22 Dec 2008	4.2	S	38	4
25 Dec 2008	4.62	S	11	1
1 Jan 2009	3.2	W	3	0
7-9 Jan 2009	5.05	S	27	2
28-29 Jan 2009	3.39	S	9	0
3 Feb 2009	3.08	E	1	0
12-13 Feb 2009	3.97	S	18	1
20 Feb 2009	3.7	W	7	1
1-2 Mar 2009	3.51	E	9	1
4 Apr 2009	3.07	SE	1	1
15 Apr 2009	3.22	SE	7	0
20-21 Apr 2009	3.03	E	2	0

Spatial Organization

The basic dichotomy of Fire Island is the separation of public land holding from private lands. There are three park entities, Federal, State, and County, on the island as well as seventeen private communities (the basic divisions are depicted on Fig. 1, and each of the individual communities are on Figs. 4-11). Each of the agencies and communities is interested in the conditions that describe its shorefront and the changes that are recorded. Therefore, this report will incorporate the outcomes of shoreline change by landholding and by community as well as the general condition of the barrier island. The intent is to document the changes that occur along the island and to track the dimensions and directions of this change. The consideration of reporting by landholding and community is a means to provide a comparative and geographical perspective to the measures of change.

Changes to the Protocol

No changes to the protocols of data collection were made during the surveys incorporated in this report.

Shoreline Position Data Sets

Following application of the protocol, each surveyed shoreline is registered to a common base and distances are measured from an offshore baseline at 10 m intervals along the baseline (see SOP # 7, Psuty, et al., 2009) (Fig. 3). The product of the first part of this procedure is a plot of the shoreline positions, the offshore baseline, and transects (Fig. 3). The second part of the procedure is a measure of the distances along the transects to each surveyed shoreline (Table 3). The complete table of measurements of distances from the baseline to the surveyed shoreline, spaced at 10 m intervals, is available from the NCBN Data Manager.

The change in shoreline position is derived from a comparison of surveyed lines and is conveyed as a measure of differences between distances at each transect location. Although the intent of the survey is to document the change in shoreline position produced by gains or losses in sediment, the shoreline position is also affected by other variables and thus there is a measure of uncertainty, or error, associated with the collected line position. There are three contributors to the variation in the estimate. Their character and dimension are: 1) the recording instrument is a GPS unit with sub-meter accuracy, its variation is about 0.3 m; 2) there is variation in the wave runup to create the neap high-tide swash line, it is 2-3 m; and 3) there is some small variation in the operator's tracking of the swash line on the beach face (0.25 m). Together, these contributors create an estimate in variation in position of +/- 2.55 m. Therefore, any surveyed shoreline has an intrinsic estimation of +/- 2.55 m. Further, any comparison between two survey lines would incorporate the estimates associated with each survey plus the variation in tidal level between the two surveys, up to 0.3 m, or an estimate of change of +/- 5.76 m, rounded to 6 m.

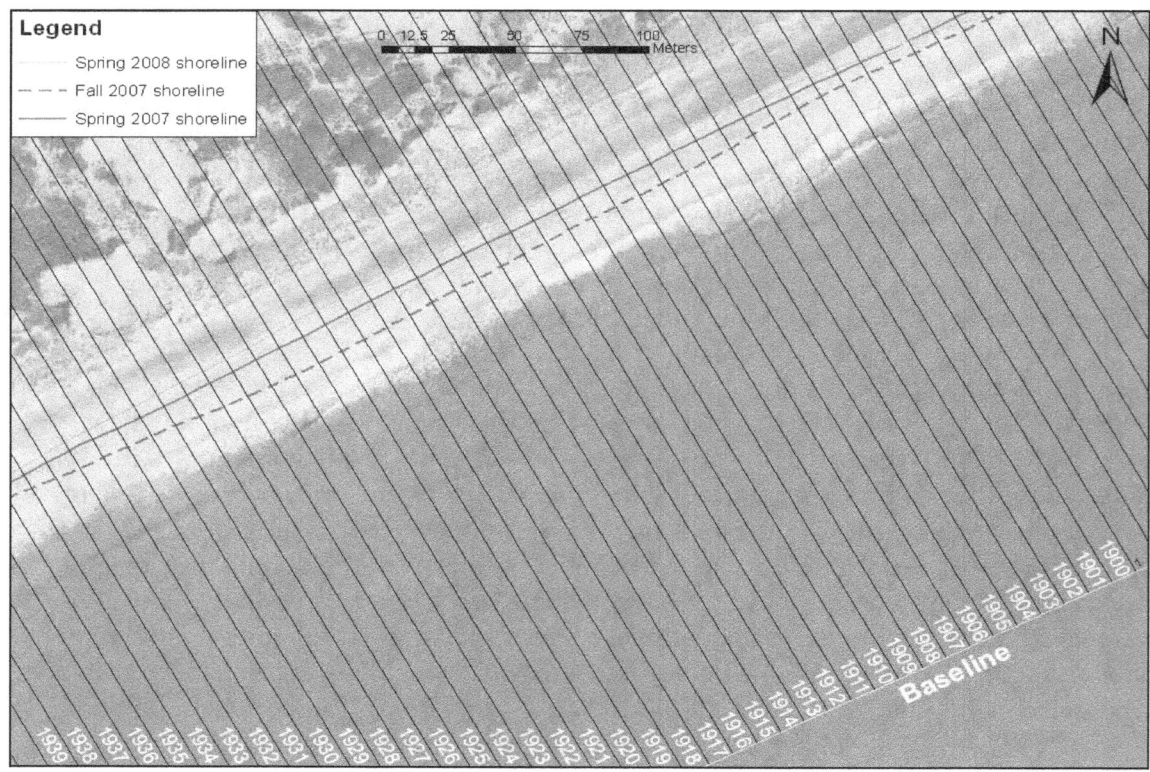

Figure 3. A sampling of surveyed shorelines intersecting with transects, and producing measures of distances from the baseline along each transect.

Table 3. A sampling of a table of measured distances from the baseline for each transect on each survey and the comparative displacements of the shoreline between surveys.

Transect Order	Distance to baseline (m) (±5m)			Changes (m) (±10m)		
	Spring 2007	Fall 2007	Spring 2008	Spring 2007 - Fall 2007	Fall 2007 - Spring 2008	Spring 2007 - Spring 2008
1900	241.78	235.92	244.99	5.86	-9.07	-3.22
1901	241.61	234.94	245.69	6.67	-10.75	-4.08
1902	241.39	234.07	246.34	7.32	-12.27	-4.95
1903	241.21	233.11	246.83	8.11	-13.72	-5.62
1904	241.03	231.96	247.05	9.07	-15.09	-6.02
1905	240.89	231.16	247.10	9.73	-15.94	-6.21
1906	240.43	230.50	247.12	9.94	-16.63	-6.69
1907	240.05	230.22	247.04	9.83	-16.82	-6.99
1908	239.78	229.77	246.78	10.01	-17.01	-7.00
1909	239.74	229.42	246.36	10.32	-16.93	-6.61
1910	239.32	229.10	245.76	10.22	-16.66	-6.44

The shoreline position measurements are reported both as seasonal changes between successive surveys and between surveys at annual intervals. In addition, the outcome of the comparison of these data sets (differences between surveys) is portrayed spatially in a series of panels (Figs. 4-11). This figure is composed of 8 pages with three panels per page. Each page is a portion of Fire Island, and each page incorporates three panels that depict the seasonal changes from Spring 2008 to Fall 2008, Fall 2008 to Spring 2009, and annual change from Spring 2008 to Spring 2009. The panels include the traces of the surveyed shorelines, a plot of the measured differences between pairs of shorelines, and a depiction of the value of the mean change and an accompanying one standard deviation for each comparison. Together, these panels incorporate the essential information on the measures and distributions of change through one year, the basis of this annual report.

A running bar graph on Figures 4-11 depicts the relative difference in shoreline position between surveys on each of the panels. Differences of less than 10 m of seaward or landward displacement (+ 10 m to -10 m) are shown as gray, whereas seaward displacement (accretion) greater than 10 m is shown as shades of blue and inland displacement (erosion) in shades of red. The tabular data of seasonal and annual differences are available from the NCBN Data Manager.

The totality of the difference measurements is also subjected to very simple statistical analysis to determine the mean and standard deviation values for the seasonal and annual comparisons. These outcomes are represented on Figures 4-11 as well in the summary tables for areas of interest. Each of the panels in these Figures has a solid black line depicting the mean difference value as well as a dotted black line representing the +/- 1.0 standard deviation value. Thus, through the incorporation of mean and standard deviation values, the spatial portrayal of change is shown relative to all other changes on the island for the same temporal span. It is a means to provide a visual perspective on the magnitude and direction of the change (vectors) on a localized basis.

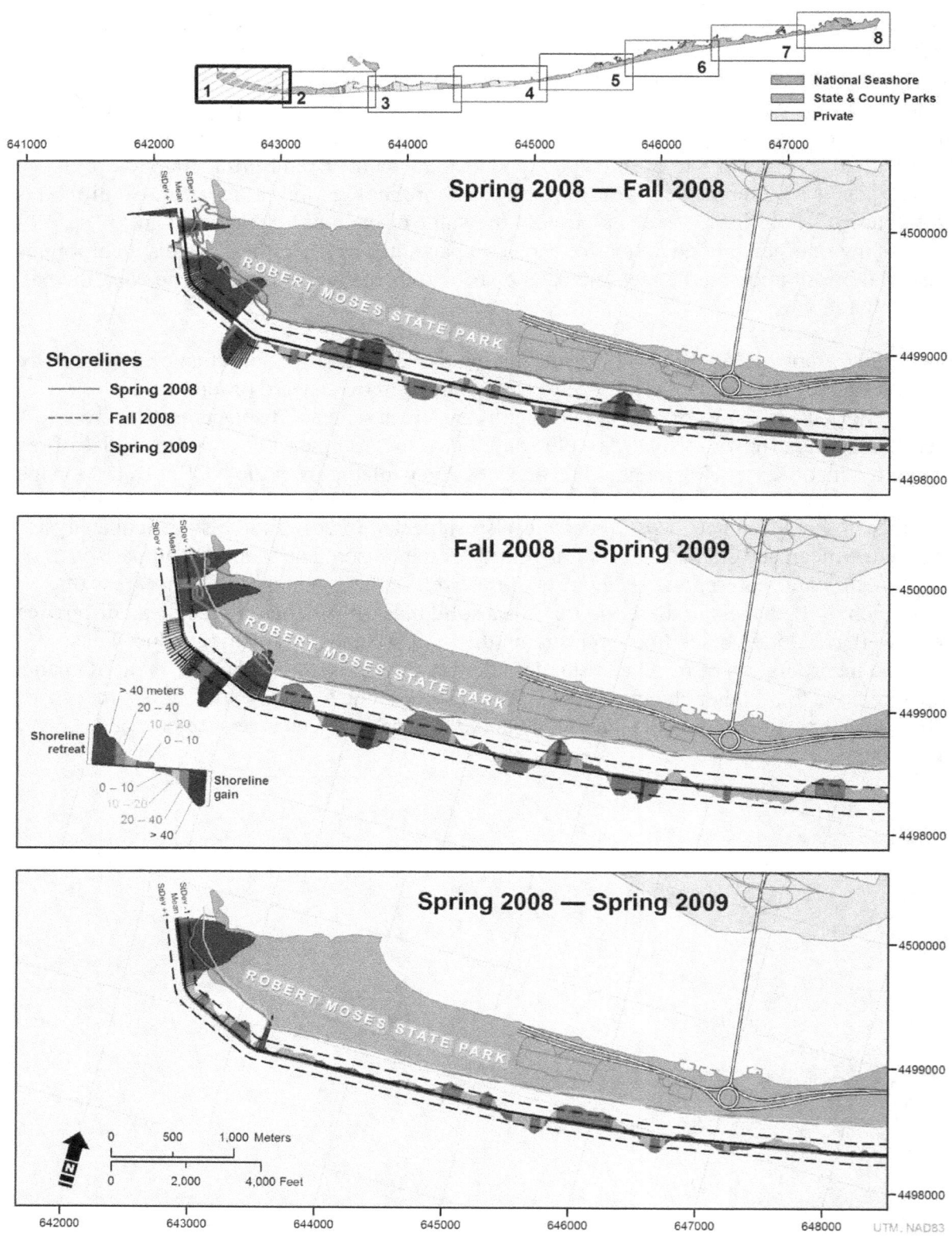

Figure 4. Distribution of seasonal and annual shoreline change values, Compartment 1, Fire Island; portrayal of magnitudes of change, mean changes, and standard deviations per temporal unit.

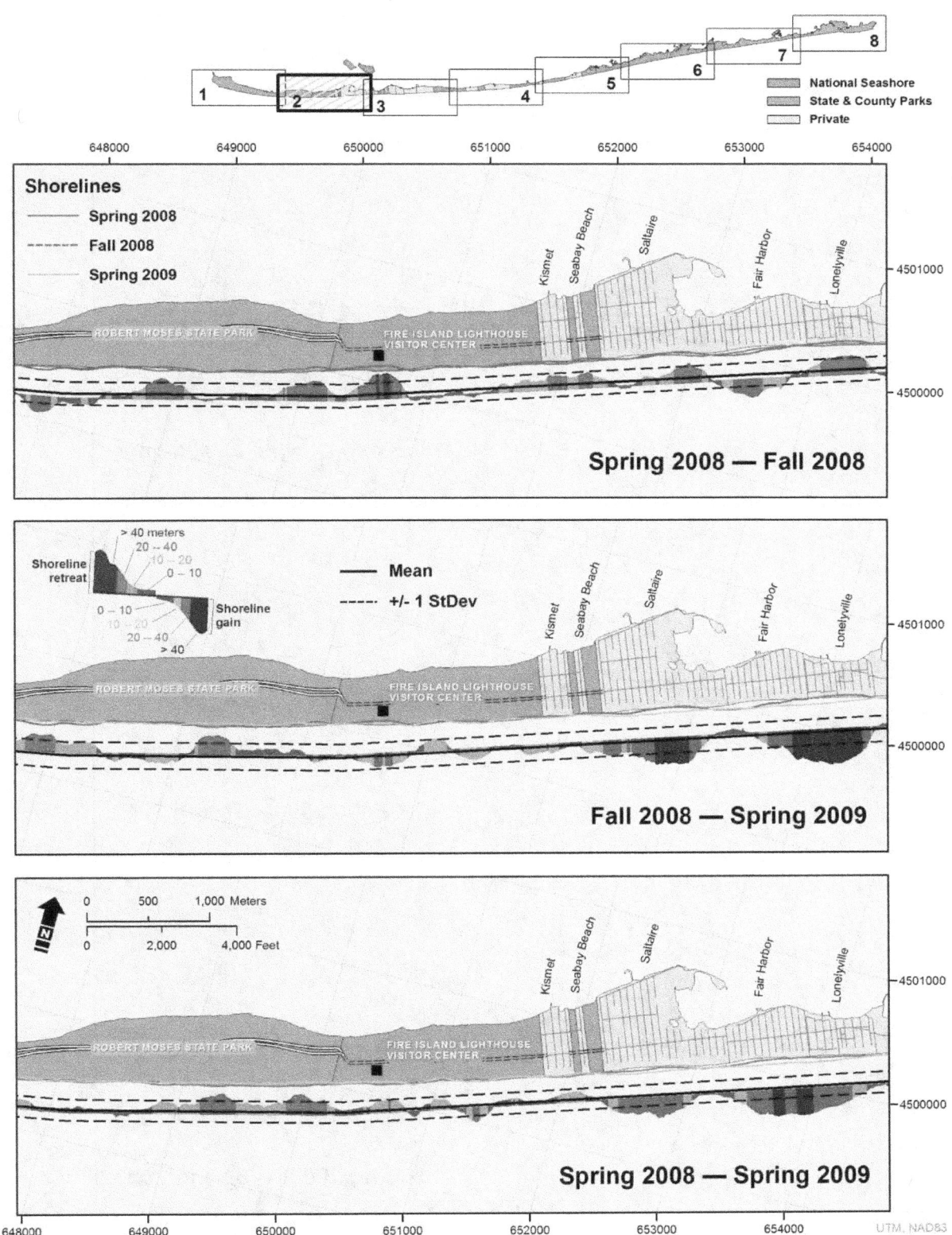

Figure 5. Distribution of seasonal and annual shoreline change values, Compartment 2, Fire Island; portrayal of magnitudes of change, mean changes, and standard deviations per temporal unit.

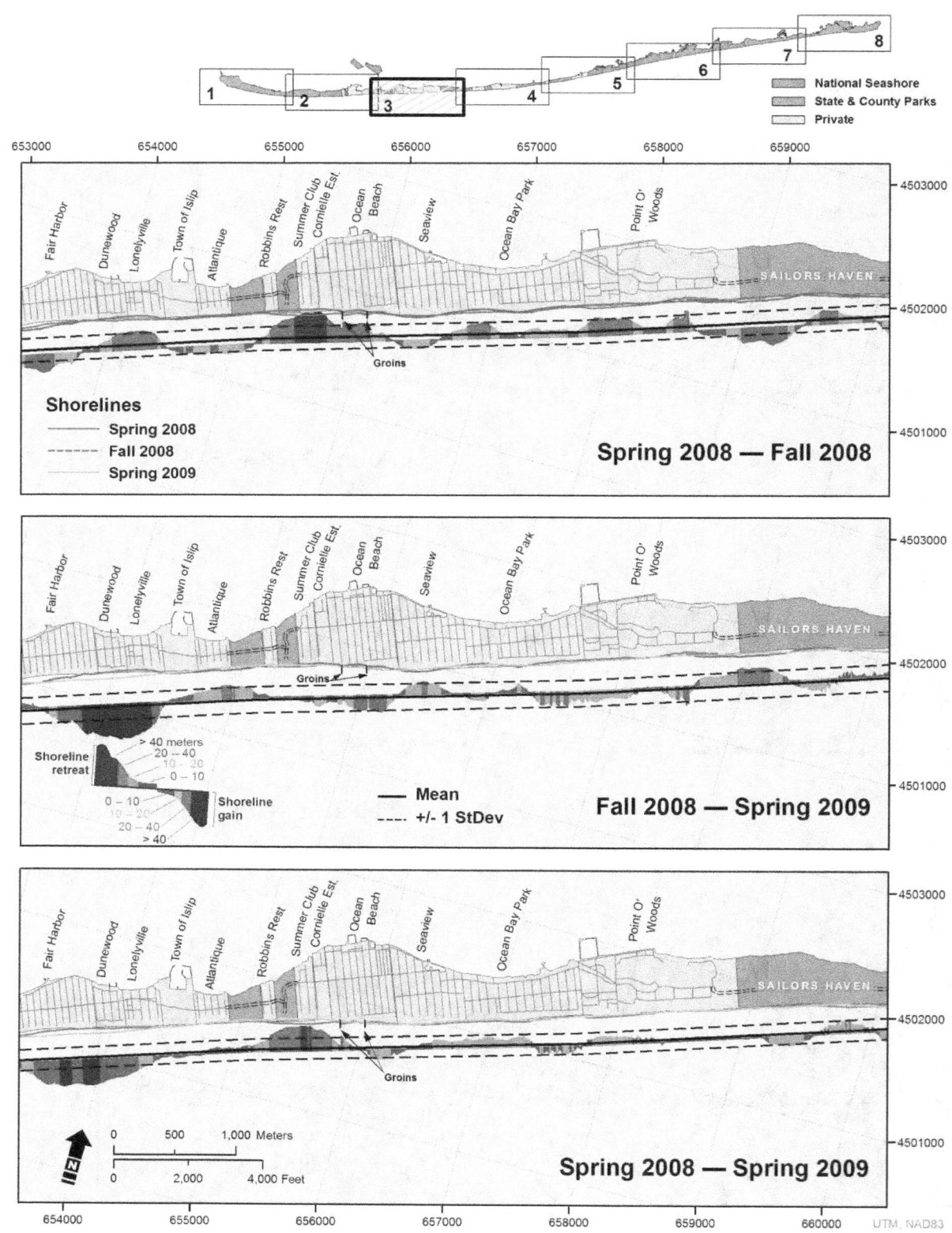

Figure 6. Distribution of seasonal and annual shoreline change values, Compartment 3, Fire Island; portrayal of magnitudes of change, mean changes, and standard deviations per temporal unit.

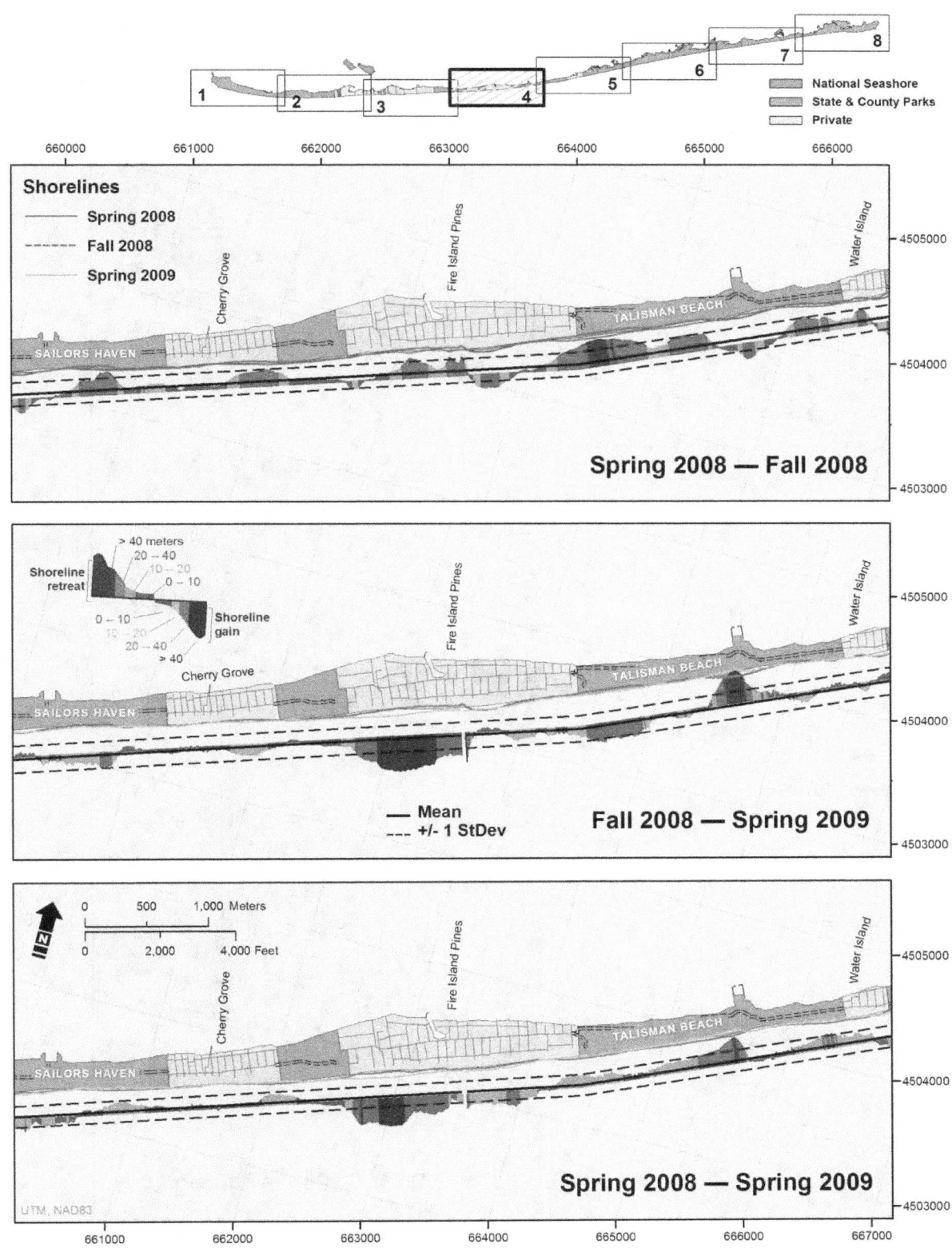

Figure 7. Distribution of seasonal and annual shoreline change values, Compartment 4, Fire Island; portrayal of magnitudes of change, mean changes, and standard deviations per temporal unit.

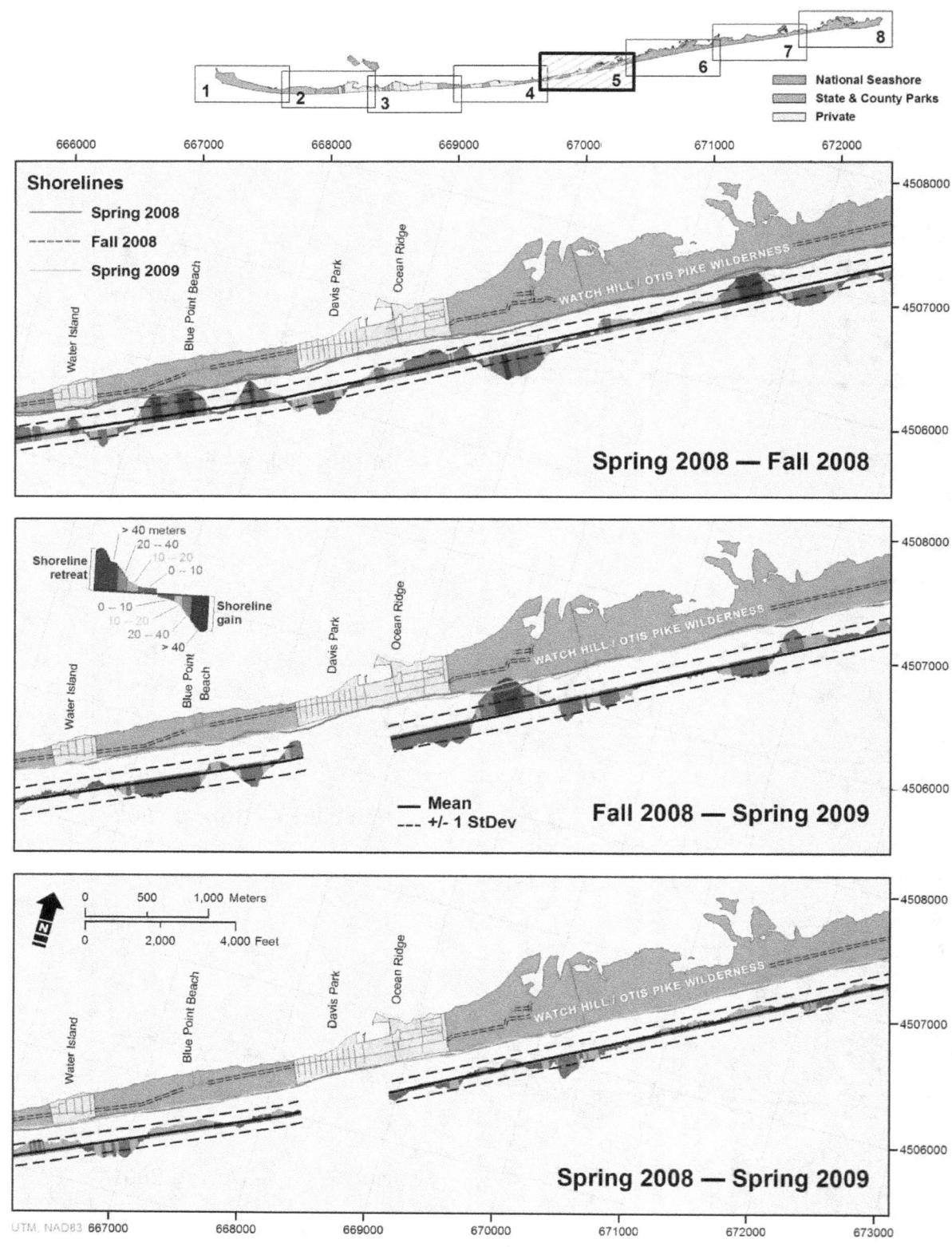

Figure 8. Distribution of seasonal and annual shoreline change values, Compartment 5, Fire Island; portrayal of magnitudes of change, mean changes, and standard deviations per temporal unit.

20

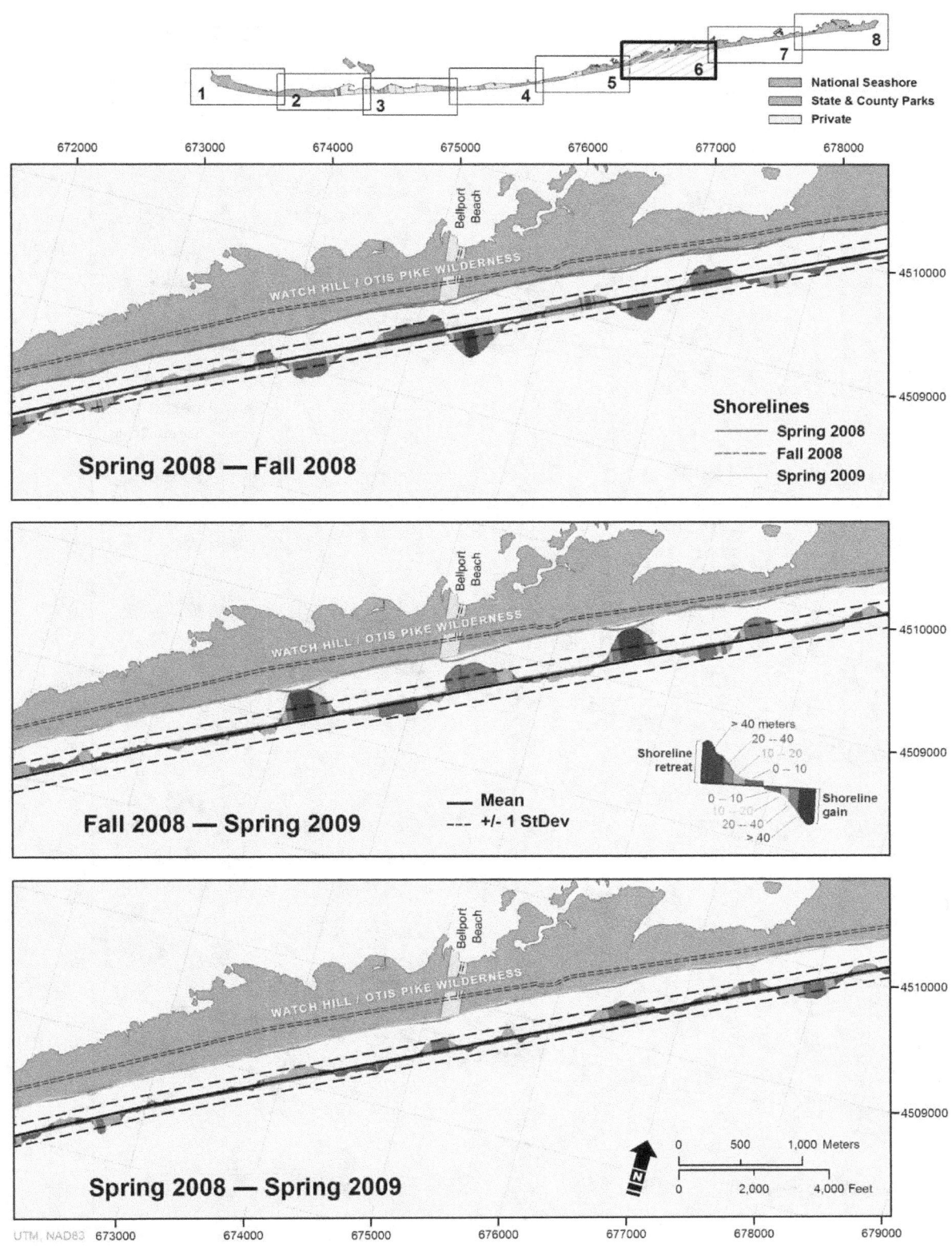

Figure 9. Distribution of seasonal and annual shoreline change values, Compartment 6, Fire Island; portrayal of magnitudes of change, mean changes, and standard deviations per temporal unit.

21

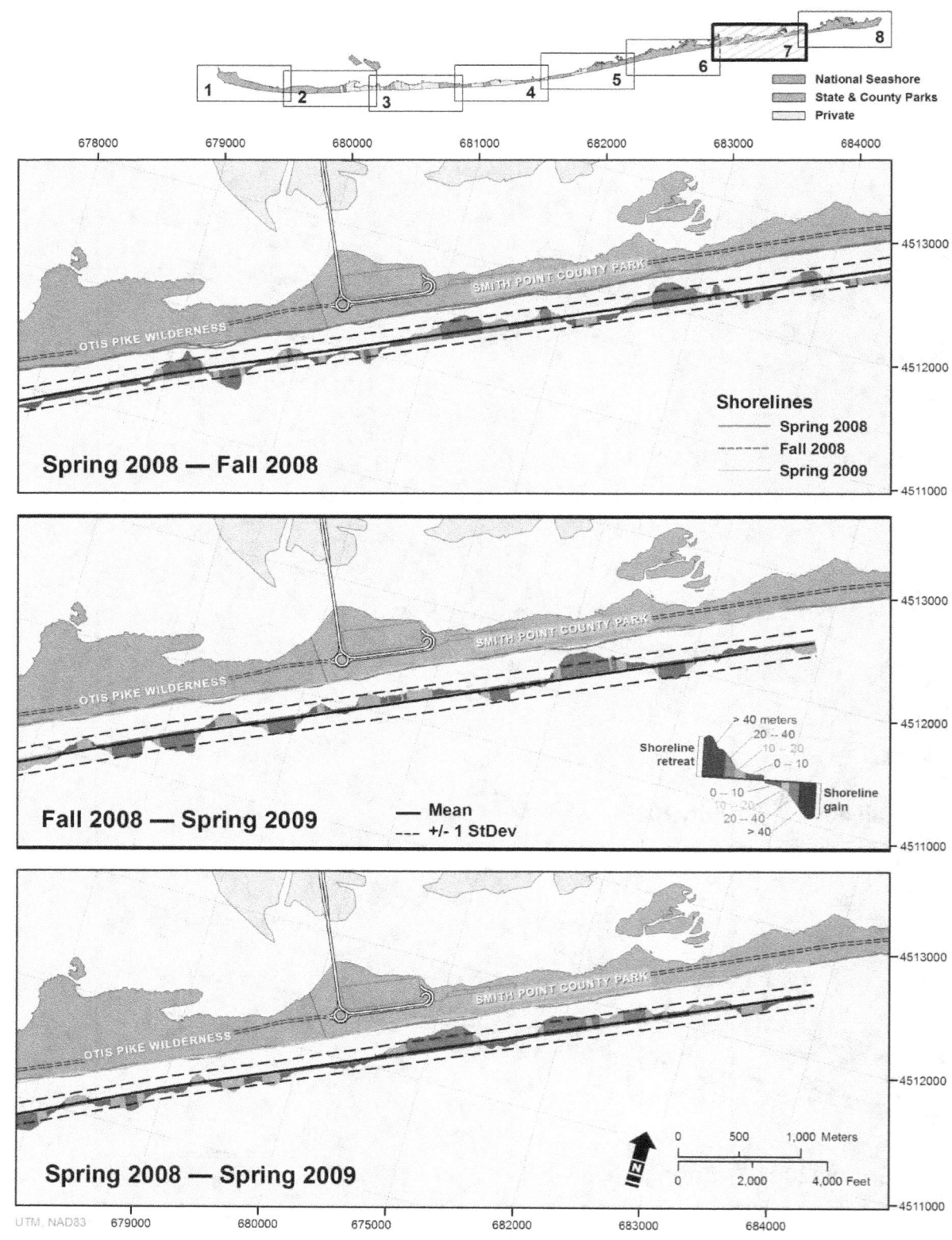

Figure 10. Distribution of seasonal and annual shoreline change values, Compartment 7, Fire Island; portrayal of magnitudes of change, mean changes, and standard deviations per temporal unit.

22

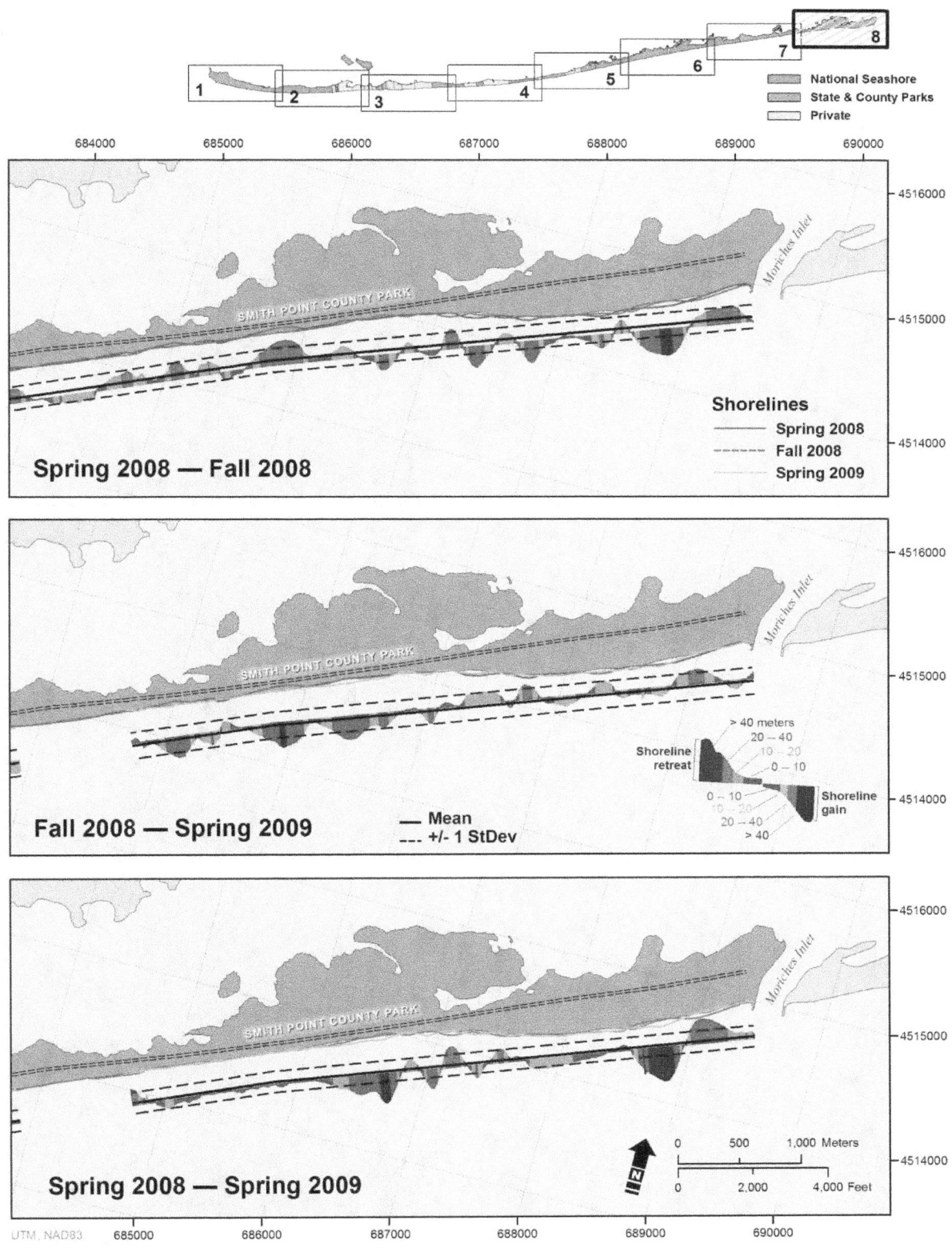

Figure 11. Distribution of seasonal and annual shoreline change values, Compartment 8, Fire Island; portrayal of magnitudes of change, mean changes, and standard deviations per temporal unit.

Spatial Analyses and Tables of Change

A general perspective of the seasonal and annual change is presented in Figure 12. It consists of three bar charts that depict the shoreline displacements in a geographical array. In addition, the differences in shoreline position are plotted in a histogram format to portray the range of the values of change (Figs. 13-15). In the seasonal comparisons as well as the annual change, there is a near normal distribution that depicts a marked central tendency in the assembled measurements and a general decline of frequency of change away from the mean values. The Fall 2008-Spring 2009 histogram is a bit different because it has a few measurements that are very large negative changes downdrift of the Fire Island Inlet jetty (Democrat Point). However, the remainder of the island is tightly grouped around a central tendency. The data are grouped in bins of 5 m; that is, each of the bars in the histograms incorporate a range of 5 m. Each histogram (Figs. 13-15) incorporates a visual portrayal of the mean value, one +/- standard deviation, and the minimum and maximum values for the survey period. The Fall 2008 – Spring 2009 changes span the beach nourishment period and have the largest positive mean value (4.07 m), whereas the Spring 2008 – Fall 2008 change has a negative mean value (-7.59 m). Over the annual period, the mean displacement is -3.66 m. Each of the seasonal changes as well as the annual change has similar and small standard deviations, ranging from 17.54 to 22.18. In each of the comparisons, the largest displacements tend to be associated with the structures at the inlets and their downdrift influences.

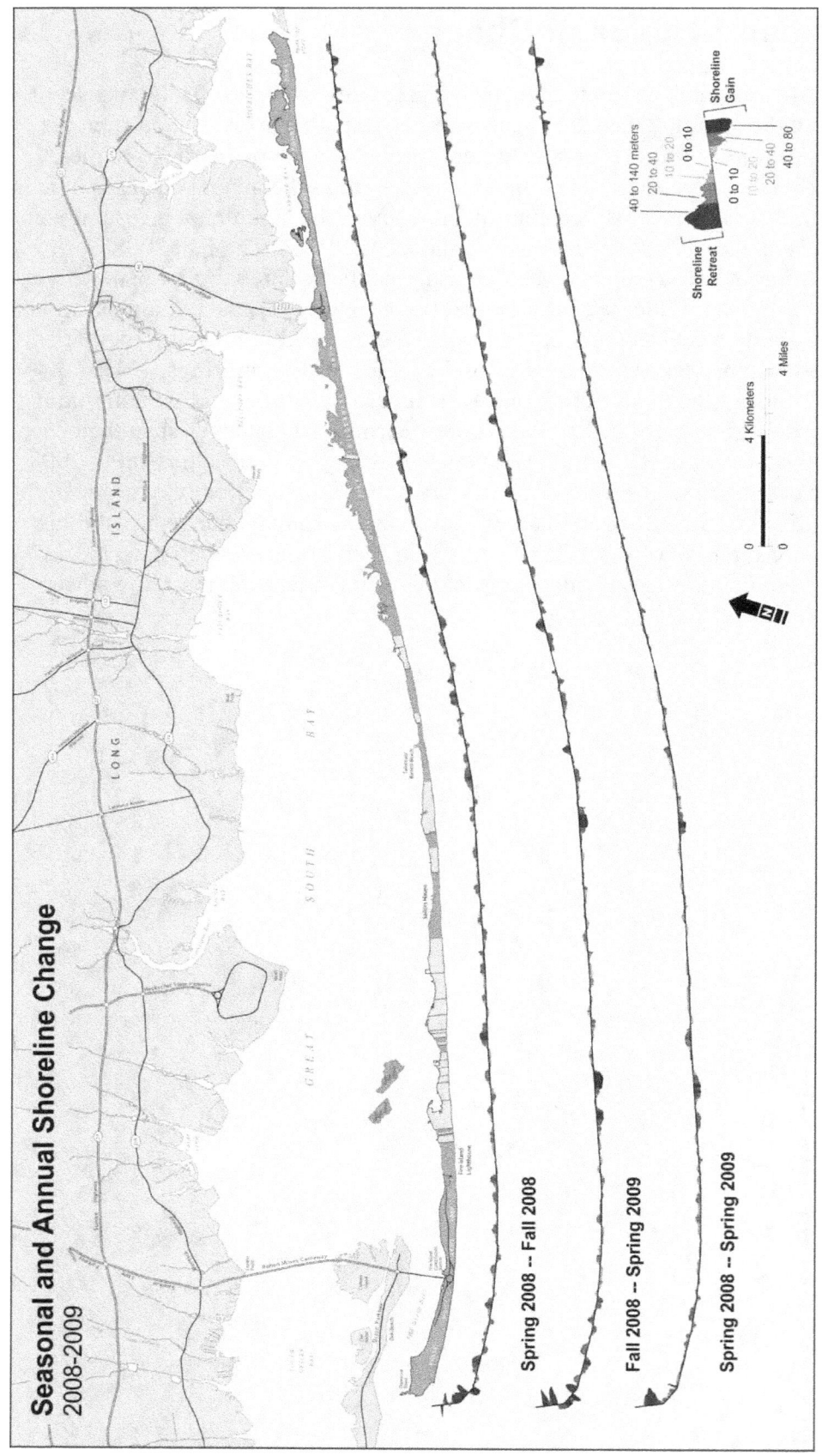

Figure 12. Alongshore distribution of changes, Spring 2008-Spring 2009.

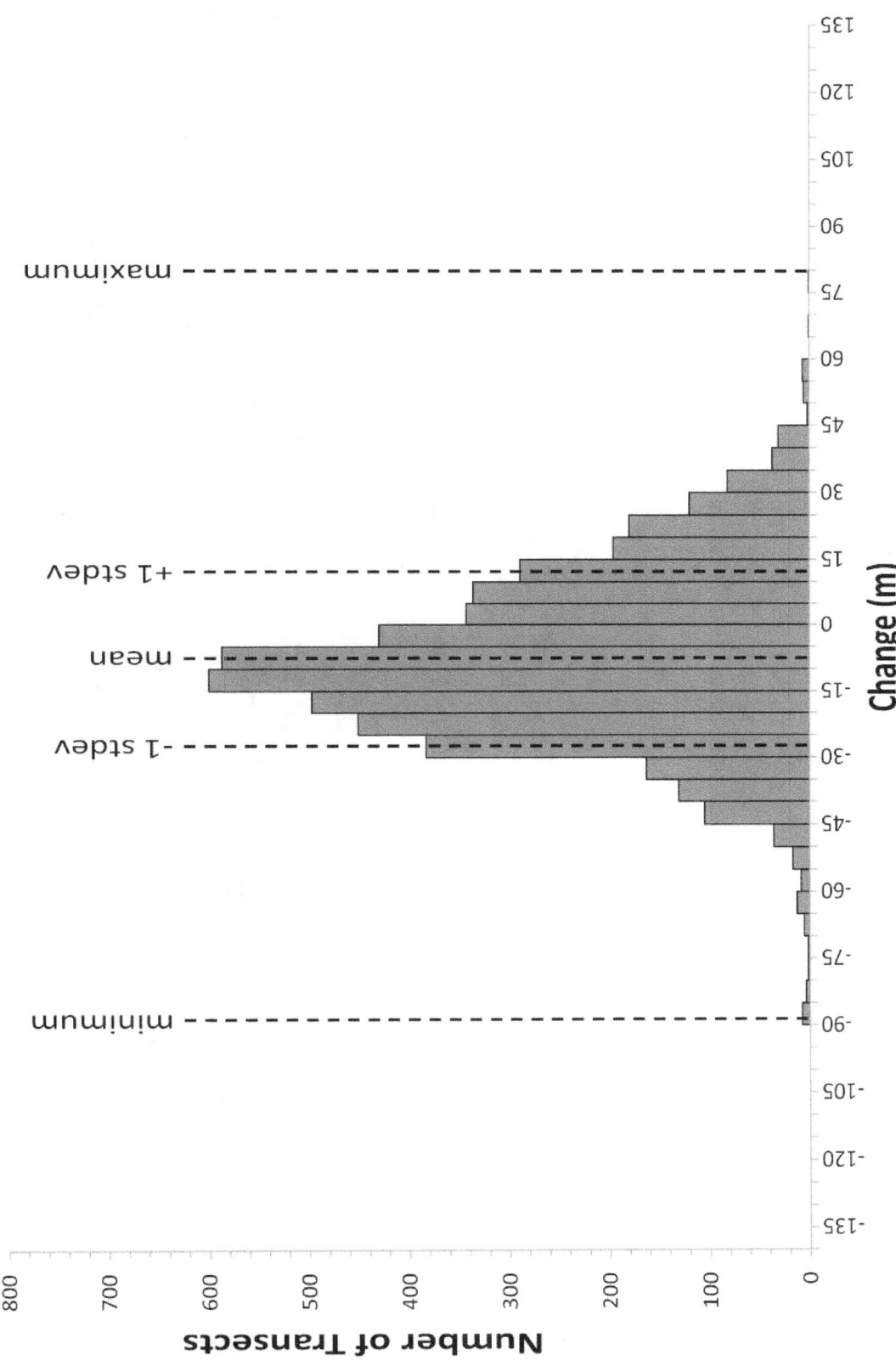

Figure 13. Distribution of difference measurements for the seasonal shoreline change between Spring 2008 and Fall 2008, incorporating the mean change value (-7.59), standard deviation (19.61), maximum (80) and minimum (-88.48).

27

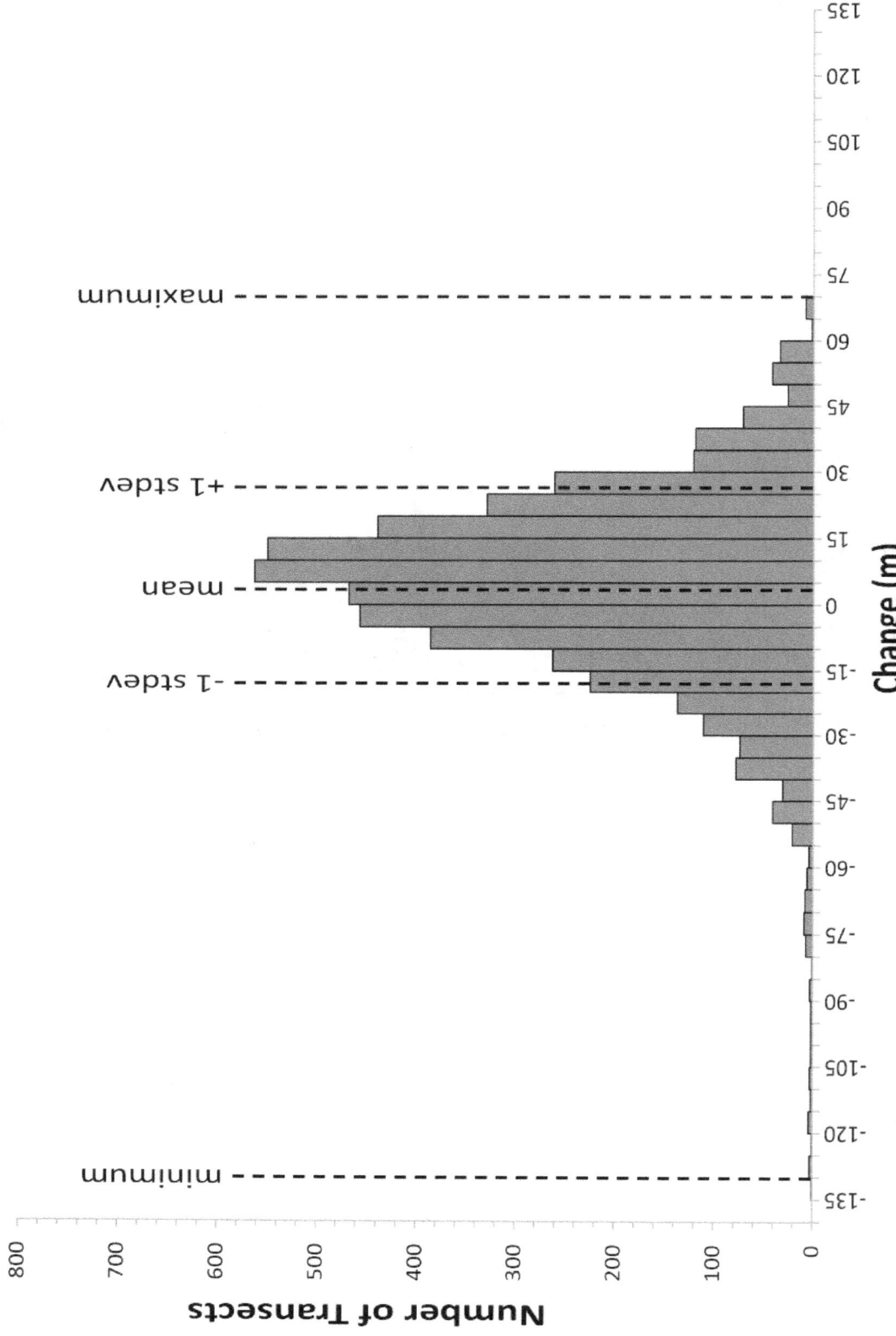

Figure 14. Distribution of difference measurements for the seasonal shoreline change between Fall 2008 and Spring 2009, incorporating the mean change value (4.07), standard deviation (22.18), maximum (69.49) and minimum (-130.31).

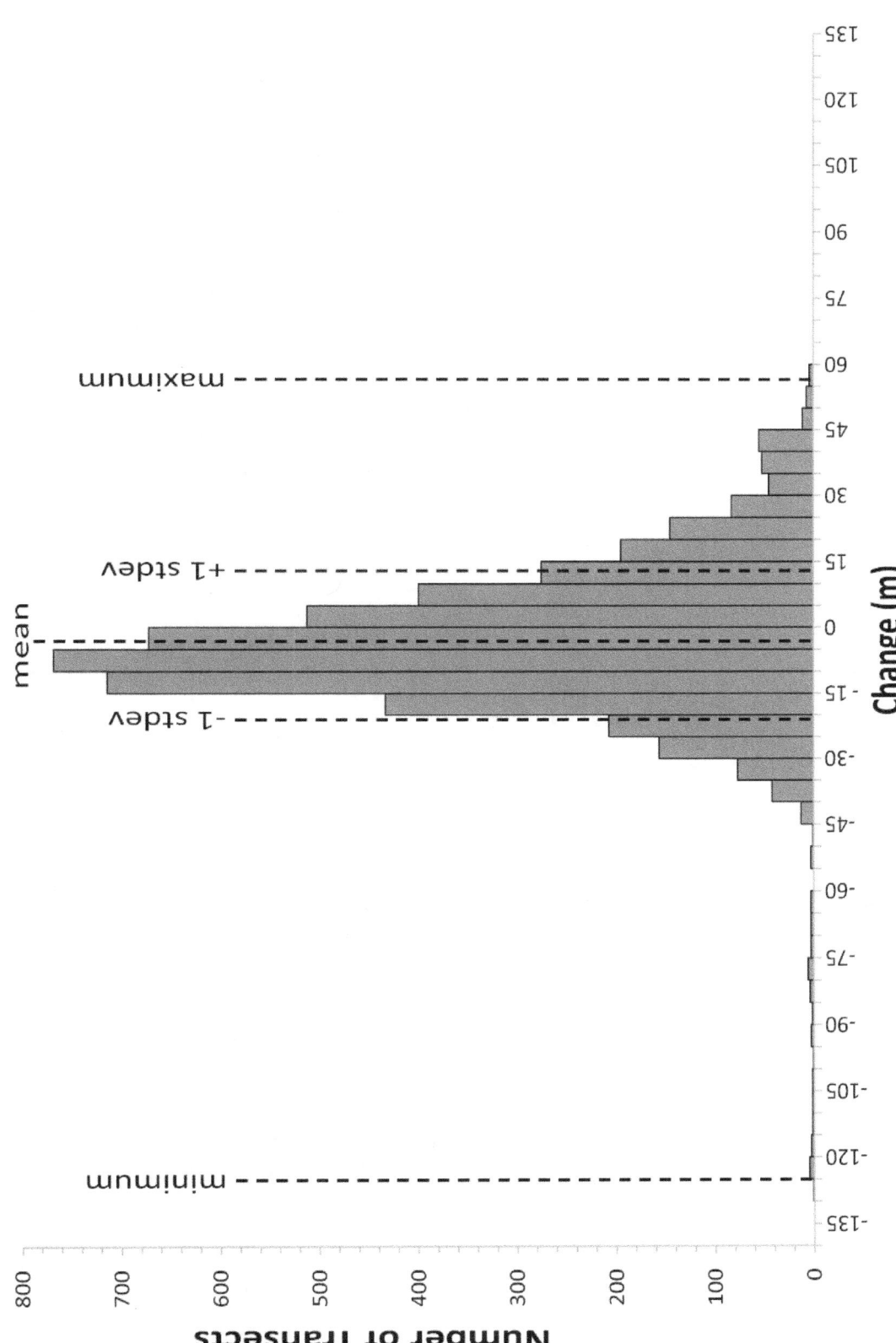

Figure 15. Distribution of difference measurements for the annual shoreline change between Spring 2008 and Spring 2009, incorporating the mean change value (-3.66), standard deviation (17.54), maximum (56.12), and minimum (-125.67).

Areas of Interest

The variety of jurisdictions and land holding on Fire Island raise interest in the rates and magnitudes of displacement along the barrier island. An initial separation of the island into Federal, State, and County holdings, plus the areas occupied by the communities reveals the similarity of shoreline displacement (Tables 4 and 5), except for locations near the jettied inlets. In Tables 4 and 5, the major divisions of the island are grouped and some are further subdivided. Thus, in Robert Moses State Park the shoreline length downdrift of the jetty at Fire Island Inlet extends 1490 m, the shoreline updrift of the jetty that is affected by the structure extends for 2560 m, and the alongshore distance in not influenced by the jetty extends for 4580 m before reaching the border of Fire Island National Seashore. Further, the portion of Smith Point County Park having a positively influenced by the Moriches Inlet jetties extends downdrift for 2660 m, the negative influence extends alongshore for 2300 m, and the portion uninfluenced by the jetty extends for 5190 m to the border with the Fire Island National Seashore. Within the zone of jetty influence, there is considerable local variation, and there is both greater positive displacement (+56.12 m) and greater negative displacement (-125.67 m) than any other place on the barrier island.

Further division of the developed area into its community compartments interspersed with public land offers another view of the comparison of rates and magnitudes of change on more local scales (Tables 6 and 7). Although there is a general consistency of change in adjacent communities, there are several trends present seasonally as well as on the annual scale, some representing the impacts of the beach nourishment episodes. It is impossible to extend the information beyond this one year, but there are observations related to the great range of shore position change as noted by the large standard deviations relative to the mean values (near the inlets), and the areas of very low standard deviations (less than 2.0 m in two NPS parcels and in two communities). The history of shoreline change on Fire Island incorporates substantial alongshore variation (Allen, et al., 2002) and this data set maintains that variation. However, this is one year and it is not prudent to ascribe longer-term changes based on this limited data set.

Table 4. Descriptive statistics of seasonal shoreline change of entire Fire Island and its major components, Spring 2008 - Fall 2009 and Fall 2009 - Spring 2010 (negative values in red).

Spatial Component	Length (m)	Spring 2008 – Fall 2008				Fall 2008 – Spring 2009			
		Mean	Stdev	Max	Min	Mean	Stdev	Max	Min
NPS land	20050	-5.39	18.69	43.42	-45.74	1.80	18.71	38.73	-54.01
Robert Moses State Park	8630	-11.61	25.62	80.00	-88.48	-4.01	32.19	69.49	-130.31
Area downdrift of jetty	1490	-24.18	47.63	80.00	-88.48	-24.21	63.07	69.49	-130.31
Area updrift and influenced by jetty	2560	-6.56	23.63	32.88	-51.32	-2.28	26.85	44.07	-64.76
Updrift, not influenced by jetty	4580	-11.13	15.43	26.51	-46.46	0.58	16.64	41.07	-30.46
Smith Point County Park	10150	-4.91	17.33	43.19	-38.81	3.01	16.37	42.20	-36.04
Area of negative inlet influence	2300	-8.74	15.14	24.29	-38.81	17.08	14.16	42.20	-13.53
Area of positive inlet influence	2660	4.36	20.96	43.19	-31.50	-2.96	12.39	16.90	-23.54
Downdrift, not influenced by inlet	5190	-7.67	14.50	22.20	-38.68	-1.08	15.11	29.52	-36.04
All developed areas	12380	-10.60	17.17	32.62	-50.14	14.63	18.72	59.27	-24.54
West of Ocean Beach groins	3420	-8.51	19.58	29.90	-50.14	18.76	22.09	59.27	-21.78
East of Ocean Beach groins	8960	-11.39	16.09	32.62	-45.24	12.92	16.85	58.10	-24.54
Total Ocean Shoreline	**51210**	-7.59	19.61	80.00	-88.48	4.07	22.18	69.49	-130.31

Table 5. Descriptive statistics of annual shoreline change of entire Fire Island and its major components, Spring 2008 – Spring 2009 (negative values in red).

Spatial Component	Length (m)	Spring 2008 – Spring 2009			
		Mean	Stdev	Max	Min
NPS land	20050	-3.61	11.78	33.45	-41.13
Robert Moses State Park	8630	-14.87	21.59	23.72	-125.67
Area downdrift of jetty	1490	-44.23	36.54	-0.95	-125.67
Area updrift and influenced by jetty	2560	-8.84	12.82	23.72	-65.03
Updrift, not influenced by jetty	4580	-10.55	12.05	23.14	-32.77
Smith Point County Park	10150	-2.26	18.17	56.12	-39.25
Area of negative inlet influence	2300	8.33	13.97	48.32	-25.44
Area of positive inlet influence	2660	1.40	22.86	56.12	-39.25
Downdrift, not influenced by inlet	5190	-10.12	12.72	14.51	-34.69
All developed areas	12380	3.20	18.15	45.17	-41.11
West of Ocean Beach groins	3420	10.25	22.01	42.44	-41.11
East of Ocean Beach groins	8960	0.27	15.36	45.17	-23.42
Total Ocean Shoreline	**51210**	-3.66	17.54	56.12	-125.67

Table 6. Descriptive statistics of seasonal shoreline change, by NPS land (shaded), and non-NPS land (unshaded), Spring 2008 – Fall 2008 and Fall 2008 – Spring 2009 (negative values in red). List reflects geographic progression along Fire Island from west to east (see Fig. 1).

Spatial Component	Length (m)	Spring 2008 - Fall 2008				Fall 2008 - Spring 2009			
		Mean	Stdev	Max	Min	Mean	Stdev	Max	Min
Robert Moses State Park	8630	-11.61	25.62	80.00	-88.48	-4.01	32.19	69.49	-130.31
NPS - Lighthouse	1720	-11.37	13.39	5.32	-41.19	6.53	10.89	21.55	-18.64
Kismet	240	-20.16	2.20	-14.87	-22.97	8.52	4.08	14.92	1.61
NPS	60	-19.39	1.40	-17.91	-21.24	4.55	2.46	8.20	1.81
Seabay Beach	60	-23.17	1.11	-22.12	-25.26	14.50	2.78	17.89	10.51
NPS	120	-18.67	3.83	-14.29	-25.32	17.48	1.42	20.08	15.59
Saltaire	1030	-9.71	11.36	14.20	-30.81	25.67	15.81	44.54	-6.46
Fair Harbor	660	13.19	12.39	29.90	-11.59	20.57	19.85	52.07	-8.50
Dunewood	230	-21.92	5.51	-12.77	-28.97	55.62	2.40	59.27	52.13
Lonelyville	310	-23.06	9.33	-1.15	-29.74	37.66	17.23	57.84	2.42
Town of Islip	270	8.23	3.57	14.10	0.04	-6.41	3.62	1.57	-12.77
Atlantique	250	11.79	2.29	14.46	8.48	-17.18	3.39	-12.49	-21.78
NPS	300	3.68	9.35	13.43	-12.09	-13.54	6.58	-3.93	-21.43
Robbins Rest	100	-24.80	5.92	-14.36	-31.28	-0.02	1.27	1.35	-2.79
NPS	180	-39.24	3.44	-32.39	-45.74	1.44	2.08	6.14	-0.93
Summer Club	160	-48.35	1.10	-46.59	-50.14	9.96	3.99	16.89	6.18
Cornielle Estates	110	-39.57	6.85	-29.54	-48.92	10.88	2.44	15.62	8.12
Ocean Beach	530	-17.94	11.29	5.82	-31.06	18.15	7.53	28.71	1.33
Seaview	570	1.42	11.76	14.29	-21.78	-8.86	9.13	6.96	-20.88
Ocean Bay Park	970	-13.12	6.38	-1.05	-26.77	8.38	10.48	23.30	-14.44
Point O'Woods	1280	-10.47	15.32	22.94	-34.28	4.18	13.44	31.54	-24.54
NPS - Sailors Haven	2410	-3.72	17.08	30.19	-36.51	2.29	12.47	24.93	-24.79
Cherry Grove	900	-12.86	8.63	0.18	-26.28	7.64	5.98	17.84	-2.44
NPS	560	-6.08	4.84	4.80	-19.77	5.44	4.61	12.27	-3.50
Fire Island Pines	1880	-7.61	16.39	22.63	-34.10	25.75	20.37	58.10	-6.43
NPS - Talisman	1780	-15.78	19.87	24.93	-42.79	1.66	22.51	31.58	-51.90
Water Island	770	-13.06	14.78	26.33	-28.73	2.54	7.53	16.82	-9.26
NPS	140	15.23	4.99	24.26	8.09	4.32	4.63	10.63	-4.66
Blue Point Beach	800	-26.30	17.97	6.93	-45.24	21.38	10.96	31.87	-10.51
NPS	730	-10.62	18.31	20.12	-43.33	4.68	19.39	38.73	-25.49
Davis Park	830	0.96	18.96	32.62	-22.85	23.89	1.44	25.05	21.13
Ocean Ridge	430	-25.68	4.06	-19.70	-32.11	27.19	5.20	36.39	20.33
NPS Watch Hill / Wilderness	12050	-2.75	18.94	43.42	-44.33	0.89	20.55	38.67	-54.01
Smith Point County Park	10150	-4.91	17.33	43.19	-38.81	3.01	16.37	42.20	-36.04

Table 7. Descriptive statistics of annual shoreline change, by NPS land (shaded) and non-NPS land (unshaded), 2008 – Spring 2009 (negative values in red). List reflects geographic progression along Fire Island from west to east (see Fig. 1).

Spatial Component	Length (m)	Spring 2008 – Spring 2009			
		Mean	Stdev	Max	Min
Robert Moses State Park	8630	-14.87	21.59	23.72	-125.67
NPS - Lighthouse	1720	-4.84	10.53	23.05	-20.12
Kismet	240	-11.64	3.71	-4.21	-16.49
NPS	60	-14.84	1.09	-13.04	-16.09
Seabay Beach	60	-8.66	1.91	-6.51	-11.61
NPS	120	-1.19	4.00	5.79	-6.62
Saltaire	1030	15.96	11.22	33.86	-4.86
Fair Harbor	660	33.75	10.44	42.44	8.65
Dunewood	230	33.70	3.34	39.88	29.08
LonelyVille	310	14.59	8.52	28.27	1.27
Town of Islip	270	1.82	1.26	3.80	-0.27
Atlantique	250	-5.39	3.77	1.79	-9.35
NPS	300	-9.85	3.15	-5.63	-16.73
Robbins Rest	100	-24.82	5.25	-17.14	-31.48
NPS	180	-37.80	2.19	-32.63	-39.62
Summer Club	160	-38.39	3.03	-32.68	-41.11
Cornielle Estates	110	-28.68	4.73	-20.44	-33.86
Ocean Beach	530	0.21	12.05	16.10	-23.42
Seaview	570	-7.44	5.99	7.95	-14.82
Ocean Bay Park	970	-4.74	10.76	12.46	-17.69
Point O'Woods	1280	-6.29	4.11	4.03	-14.07
NPS - Sailors Haven	2410	-1.43	10.94	20.47	-21.47
Cherry Grove	900	-5.22	5.32	3.47	-16.98
NPS	560	-0.64	8.20	15.62	-14.32
Fire Island Pines	1880	18.47	17.42	45.17	-19.38
NPS - Talisman	1780	-14.11	10.04	3.65	-41.13
Water Island	770	-10.52	10.49	18.67	-23.38
NPS	140	19.54	1.46	22.07	16.91
Blue Point Beach	800	-4.92	13.86	25.53	-16.54
NPS	730	-6.32	4.74	4.40	-14.84
Davis Park	830	7.75	1.42	9.74	5.31
Ocean Ridge	430	1.51	6.51	15.61	-6.30
NPS Watch Hill / Wilderness	12050	-1.86	11.17	33.45	-27.98
Smith Point County Park	10150	-2.26	18.17	56.12	-39.25

Conclusions and Information for Management

With the caveat that the data presented only apply to a one-year period, there are many locations that have changes greater than +/- 6 m measure of uncertainly and a proportion that are greater than the one-standard-deviation. Both inlet areas, at the margins of Robert Moses State Park and Smith Point County Park, have large inland displacements. Longer term tendencies of shoreline change will be the analyzed through the 5-years Trend Reports.

Problems/Concerns

There was one issue that arose in this period because of the beach nourishment operation. A portion of Davis Park could not be surveyed because of nourishment activity. That void affects the statistics describing Davis Park and all of the other groupings of communities. Another small matter was the potential for loss of satellite communication during the survey, especially from around noon to 1 pm. It is necessary to check the GPS unit regularly to determine the efficacy of the connection and the collection of shoreline position, as per the protocol.

Data Availability

The lines that represent the shoreline position for each of the surveyed periods are stored as shapefiles in a Geodatabase along with the Transects, the Baseline used in the shoreline change analysis, and the spreadsheet with the results from the DSAS analysis. This information and data are available from the Data Manager for the National Park Service, Northeast Coastal and Barrier Network, Inventory and Monitoring Program:

National Park Service
Northeast Coastal and Barrier Network
University of Rhode Island
Rm. 105, 1 Greenhouse Rd.
Kingston, RI 02881

Literature Cited

Allen, J. R., C. LaBash, P. August, and N. Psuty. 2002. Historical and recent shoreline changes, impacts of Moriches Inlet, and relevance to Long Island breaching at Fire Island National Seashore, NY. Technical Report NPS/BSO-RNR/NRTR/2002-7. Dept. of the Interior, National Park Service. Available at: http://www.nps.gov/nero/science/FINAL/FIIS_shoreline/FIIS_shoreline.htm (accessed 19 December 2011).

National Oceanic and Atmospheric Administration, 2009. The Center for Operational Oceanographic Products and Services. Available at: http://tidesandcurrents.noaa.gov/ (accessed 19 December 2011).

Psuty, N. P., M. Grace, and J. P. Pace. September 2005. The coastal geomorphology of Fire Island: A portrait of continuity and change (Fire Island National Seashore Science Synthesis Paper). Technical Report NPS/NER/NRTR—2005/021. National Park Service. Boston, MA. 70 p. Available at: http://www.nps.gov/nero/science/ (accessed 19 December 2011).

Psuty, N. P., M. Duffy, J. F. Pace, D. E. Skidds, and T. M. Silveira. December 2009. Northeast Coastal and Barrier Network geomorphological monitoring protocol: Part I—ocean shoreline position. Natural Resource Report NPS/HTLN/NRR - 2009/xxx. National Park Service, Fort Collins, Colorado.

NPS 615/111995, December 2011